# All My Pretty Ones

Also by Anne Sexton

To Bedlam and Part Way Back

ANNE SEXTON

# All My Pretty Ones

"All my pretty ones?
Did you say all? O hell-kite! All?
What! all my pretty chickens and their dam
At one fell swoop? . . .
I cannot but remember such things were,
That were most precious to me.

*Macbeth*

HOUGHTON MIFFLIN COMPANY BOSTON

THE RIVERSIDE PRESS CAMBRIDGE

FOURTH PRINTING     R

Copyright © 1961, 1962 by Anne Sexton
Copyright © 1961 by Harper & Brothers
All rights reserved including the right to
reproduce this book or parts thereof in any form
Library of Congress Catalog Card Number: 62–14201

𝕿𝖍𝖊 𝕽𝖎𝖛𝖊𝖗𝖘𝖎𝖉𝖊 𝕻𝖗𝖊𝖘𝖘
Cambridge · Massachusetts
Printed in the U.S.A.

# ACKNOWLEDGMENTS

I wish to thank the Radcliffe Institute for Independent Study for their financial support and their belief in this book, and the editors of the following magazines and anthologies in which certain of the poems in this volume have previously appeared:

*The Complete Partisan Reader,* edited by William Phillips and Philip Rahv:  In the Deep Museum

*Harper's Magazine:*  To a Friend Whose Work Has Come to Triumph

*The Hudson Review:*  The Truth the Dead Know; All My Pretty Ones; Young; Old Dwarf Heart; I Remember; The Operation; The Hangman; Doors, Doors, Doors; Love Song for K. Owyne; Letter Written During a January Northeaster

*The Literary Review:*  Lament

*Modern American Poetry,* edited by Louis Untermeyer: The Truth the Dead Know, In the Deep Museum

*The Modern American Poets,* edited by John Malcolm Brinnin and Bill Read:  Letter Written on a Ferry While Crossing Long Island Sound

*The Nation:*  The Starry Night

*The New Poets of England and America: Second Selection,* edited by Donald Hall and Robert Pack:  The Truth the Dead Know, For God While Sleeping

*The New Yorker:*  The Fortress, Letter Written on a Ferry While Crossing Long Island Sound

*Partisan Review:*  A Curse Against Elegies, The Abortion, With Mercy for the Greedy, For God While Sleeping, In the Deep Museum, Ghosts

*Poetry* (Chicago):  Old, Woman with Girdle, The House, Water, Wallflower, From the Garden, For Eleanor Boylan Talking with God, The Black Art

*Supplement of American Poetry,* edited by W. S. Merwin (The Poetry Book Society, London):  Flight

A.S.

. . . the books we need are the kind that act
upon us like a misfortune, that make us suffer
like the death of someone we love more than
ourselves, that make us feel as though we were
on the verge of suicide, or lost in a forest remote
from all human habitation — a book should serve
as the ax for the frozen sea within us.

from a letter of FRANZ KAFKA
to OSKAR POLLAK

# CONTENTS

## 1

## 2

1

# THE TRUTH THE DEAD KNOW

For my mother, born March 1902, died March 1959
and my father, born February 1900, died June 1959


Gone, I say and walk from church,
refusing the stiff procession to the grave,
letting the dead ride alone in the hearse.
It is June. I am tired of being brave.

We drive to the Cape. I cultivate
myself where the sun gutters from the sky,
where the sea swings in like an iron gate
and we touch. In another country people die.

My darling, the wind falls in like stones
from the whitehearted water and when we touch
we enter touch entirely. No one's alone.
Men kill for this, or for as much.

And what of the dead? They lie without shoes
in their stone boats. They are more like stone
than the sea would be if it stopped. They refuse
to be blessed, throat, eye and knucklebone.

# ALL MY PRETTY ONES

Father, this year's jinx rides us apart
where you followed our mother to her cold slumber;
a second shock boiling its stone to your heart,
leaving me here to shuffle and disencumber
you from the residence you could not afford:
a gold key, your half of a woolen mill,
twenty suits from Dunne's, an English Ford,
the love and legal verbiage of another will,
boxes of pictures of people I do not know.
I touch their cardboard faces. They must go.

But the eyes, as thick as wood in this album,
hold me. I stop here, where a small boy
waits in a ruffled dress for someone to come . . .
for this soldier who holds his bugle like a toy
or for this velvet lady who cannot smile.
Is this your father's father, this commodore
in a mailman suit? My father, time meanwhile
has made it unimportant who you are looking for.
I'll never know what these faces are all about.
I lock them into their book and throw them out.

This is the yellow scrapbook that you began
the year I was born; as crackling now and wrinkly
as tobacco leaves: clippings where Hoover outran
the Democrats, wiggling his dry finger at me
and Prohibition; news where the *Hindenburg* went
down and recent years where you went flush

on war.  This year, solvent but sick, you meant
to marry that pretty widow in a one-month rush.
But before you had that second chance, I cried
on your fat shoulder.  Three days later you died.

These are the snapshots of marriage, stopped in places.
Side by side at the rail toward Nassau now;
here, with the winner's cup at the speedboat races,
here, in tails at the Cotillion, you take a bow,
here, by our kennel of dogs with their pink eyes,
running like show-bred pigs in their chain-link pen;
here, at the horseshow where my sister wins a prize;
and here, standing like a duke among groups of men.
Now I fold you down, my drunkard, my navigator,
my first lost keeper, to love or look at later.

I hold a five-year diary that my mother kept
for three years, telling all she does not say
of your alcoholic tendency.  You overslept,
she writes.  My God, father, each Christmas Day
with your blood, will I drink down your glass
of wine?  The diary of your hurly-burly years
goes to my shelf to wait for my age to pass.
Only in this hoarded span will love persevere.
Whether you are pretty or not, I outlive you,
bend down my strange face to yours and forgive you.

# YOUNG

A thousand doors ago
when I was a lonely kid
in a big house with four
garages and it was summer
as long as I could remember,
I lay on the lawn at night,
clover wrinkling under me,
the wise stars bedding over me,
my mother's window a funnel
of yellow heat running out,
my father's window, half shut,
an eye where sleepers pass,
and the boards of the house
were smooth and white as wax
and probably a million leaves
sailed on their strange stalks
as the crickets ticked together
and I, in my brand new body,
which was not a woman's yet,
told the stars my questions
and thought God could really see
the heat and the painted light,
elbows, knees, dreams, goodnight.

# LAMENT

Someone is dead.
Even the trees know it,
those poor old dancers who come on lewdly,
all pea-green scarfs and spine pole.
I think . . .
I think I could have stopped it,
if I'd been as firm as a nurse
or noticed the neck of the driver
as he cheated the crosstown lights;
or later in the evening,
if I'd held my napkin over my mouth.
I think I could . . .
if I'd been different, or wise, or calm,
I think I could have charmed the table,
the stained dish or the hand of the dealer.
But it's done.
It's all used up.
There's no doubt about the trees
spreading their thin feet into the dry grass.
A Canada goose rides up,
spread out like a gray suede shirt,
honking his nose into the March wind.
In the entryway a cat breathes calmly
into her watery blue fur.
The supper dishes are over and the sun
unaccustomed to anything else
goes all the way down.

# TO A FRIEND WHOSE WORK HAS COME TO TRIUMPH

Consider Icarus, pasting those sticky wings on,
testing that strange little tug at his shoulder blade,
and think of that first flawless moment over the lawn
of the labyrinth. Think of the difference it made!
There below are the trees, as awkward as camels;
and here are the shocked starlings pumping past
and think of innocent Icarus who is doing quite well:
larger than a sail, over the fog and the blast
of the plushy ocean, he goes. Admire his wings!
Feel the fire at his neck and see how casually
he glances up and is caught, wondrously tunneling
into that hot eye. Who cares that he fell back to the sea?
See him acclaiming the sun and come plunging down
while his sensible daddy goes straight into town.

# THE STARRY NIGHT

*That does not keep me from having a terrible need of — shall I say the word — religion. Then I go out at night to paint the stars.*
    VINCENT VAN GOGH in a letter to his brother


The town does not exist
except where one black-haired tree slips
up like a drowned woman into the hot sky.
The town is silent. The night boils with eleven stars.
Oh starry starry night! This is how
I want to die.

It moves. They are all alive.
Even the moon bulges in its orange irons
to push children, like a god, from its eye.
The old unseen serpent swallows up the stars.
Oh starry starry night! This is how
I want to die:

into that rushing beast of the night,
sucked up by that great dragon, to split
from my life with no flag,
no belly,
no cry.

# OLD DWARF HEART

True. All too true. I have never been at home in
life. All my decay has taken place upon a child.
    *Henderson the Rain King*, by SAUL BELLOW

When I lie down to love,
old dwarf heart shakes her head.
Like an imbecile she was born old.
Her eyes wobble as thirty-one thick folds
of skin open to glare at me on my flickering bed.
She knows the decay we're made of.

When hurt she is abrupt.
Now she is solid, like fat,
breathing in loops like a green hen
in the dust. But if I dream of loving, then
my dreams are of snarling strangers. *She* dreams that . . .
strange, strange, and corrupt.

Good God, the things she knows!
And worse, the sores she holds
in her hands, gathered in like a nest
from an abandoned field. At her best
she is all red muscle, humming in and out, cajoled
by time. Where I go, she goes.

Oh now I lay me down to love,
how awkwardly her arms undo,
how patiently I untangle her wrists
like knots. Old ornament, old naked fist,
even if I put on seventy coats I could not cover you . . .
mother, father, I'm made of.

# I  REMEMBER

By the first of August
the invisible beetles began
to snore and the grass was
as tough as hemp and was
no color — no more than
the sand was a color and
we had worn our bare feet
bare since the twentieth
of June and there were times
we forgot to wind up your
alarm clock and some nights
we took our gin warm and neat
from old jelly glasses while
the sun blew out of sight
like a red picture hat and
one day I tied my hair back
with a ribbon and you said
that I looked almost like
a puritan lady and what
I remember best is that
the door to your room was
the door to mine.

# THE OPERATION

After the sweet promise,
the summer's mild retreat
from mother's cancer, the winter months of her death,
I come to this white office, its sterile sheet,
its hard tablet, its stirrups, to hold my breath
while I, who must, allow the glove its oily rape,
to hear the almost mighty doctor over me equate
my ills with hers
and decide to operate.

It grew in her
as simply as a child would grow,
as simply as she housed me once, fat and female.
Always my most gentle house before that embryo
of evil spread in her shelter and she grew frail.
Frail, we say, remembering fear, that face we wear
in the room of the special smells of dying, fear
where the snoring mouth gapes
and is not dear.

There was snow everywhere.
Each day I grueled through
its sloppy peak, its blue-struck days, my boots
slapping into the hospital halls, past the retinue
of nurses at the desk, to murmur in cahoots
with hers outside her door, to enter with the outside
air stuck on my skin, to enter smelling her pride,
her upkeep, and to lie
as all who love have lied.

No reason to be afraid,
my almost mighty doctor reasons.
I nod, thinking that woman's dying
must come in seasons,
thinking that living is worth buying.
I walk out, scuffing a raw leaf,
kicking the clumps of dead straw
that were this summer's lawn.
Automatically I get in my car,
knowing the historic thief
is loose in my house
and must be set upon.


2.


Clean of the body's hair,
I lie smooth from breast to leg.
All that was special, all that was rare
is common here.  Fact: death too is in the egg.
Fact: the body is dumb, the body is meat.
And tomorrow the O.R.  Only the summer was sweet.

The rooms down the hall are calling
all night long, while the night outside
sucks at the trees.  I hear limbs falling
and see yellow eyes flick in the rain.  Wide eyed
and still whole I turn in my bin like a shorn lamb.
A nurse's flashlight blinds me to see who I am.

The walls color in a wash
of daylight until the room takes its objects
into itself again.  I smoke furtively and squash
the butt and hide it with my watch and other effects.
The halls bustle with legs.  I smile at the nurse
who smiles for the morning shift.  Day is worse.

Scheduled late, I cannot drink
or eat, except for yellow pills
and a jigger of water. I wait and think
until she brings two mysterious needles: the skills
she knows she knows, promising, soon you'll be out.
But nothing is sure. No one. I wait in doubt.


I wait like a kennel of dogs
jumping against their fence. At ten
she returns, laughs and catalogues
my resistance to drugs. On the stretcher, citizen
and boss of my own body still, I glide down the halls
and rise in the iron cage toward science and pitfalls.


The great green people stand
over me; I roll on the table
under a terrible sun, following their command
to curl, head touching knee if I am able.
Next, I am hung up like a saddle and they begin.
Pale as an angel I float out over my own skin.


I soar in hostile air
over the pure women in labor,
over the crowning heads of babies being born.
I plunge down the backstair
calling *mother* at the dying door,
to rush back to my own skin, tied where it was torn.
Its nerves pull like wires
snapping from the leg to the rib.
Strangers, their faces rolling like hoops, require
my arm. I am lifted into my aluminum crib.

3.

Skull flat, here in my harness,
thick with shock, I call mother
to help myself, call toe of frog,
that woolly bat, that tongue of dog;
call God help and all the rest.
The soul that swam the furious water
sinks now in flies and the brain
flops like a docked fish and the eyes
are flat boat decks riding out the pain.

My nurses, those starchy ghosts,
hover over me for my lame hours
and my lame days. The mechanics
of the body pump for their tricks.
I rest on their needles, am dosed
and snoring amid the orange flowers
and the eyes of visitors. I wear,
like some senile woman, a scarlet
candy package ribbon in my hair.

Four days from home I lurk on my
mechanical parapet with two pillows
at my elbows, as soft as praying cushions.
My knees work with the bed that runs
on power. I grumble to forget the lie
I ought to hear, but don't. God knows
I thought I'd die — but here I am,
recalling mother, the sound of her
good morning, the odor of orange and jam.

All's well, they say. They say I'm better.
I lounge in frills or, picturesque,
I wear bunny pink slippers in the hall.
I read a new book and shuffle past the desk

to mail the author my first fan letter.
Time now to pack this humpty-dumpty
back the frightened way she came
and run along, Anne, and run along now,
my stomach laced up like a football
for the game.

I want no pallid humanitarianism
— If Christ be not God, I want
none of him; I will hack my way
through existence alone . . .

GUARDINI

# A CURSE AGAINST ELEGIES

Oh, love, why do we argue like this?
I am tired of all your pious talk.
Also, I am tired of all the dead.
They refuse to listen,
so leave them alone.
Take your foot out of the graveyard,
they are busy being dead.

Everyone was always to blame:
the last empty fifth of booze,
the rusty nails and chicken feathers
that stuck in the mud on the back doorstep,
the worms that lived under the cat's ear
and the thin-lipped preacher
who refused to call
except once on a flea-ridden day
when he came scuffing in through the yard
looking for a scapegoat.
I hid in the kitchen under the ragbag.

I refuse to remember the dead.
And the dead are bored with the whole thing.
But you — you go ahead,
go on, go on back down
into the graveyard,
lie down where you think their faces are;
talk back to your old bad dreams.

# THE ABORTION

*Somebody who should have been born*
*is gone.*

Just as the earth puckered its mouth,
each bud puffing out from its knot,
I changed my shoes, and then drove south.

Up past the Blue Mountains, where
Pennsylvania humps on endlessly,
wearing, like a crayoned cat, its green hair,

its roads sunken in like a gray washboard;
where, in truth, the ground cracks evilly,
a dark socket from which the coal has poured,

*Somebody who should have been born*
*is gone.*

the grass as bristly and stout as chives,
and me wondering when the ground would break,
and me wondering how anything fragile survives;

up in Pennsylvania, I met a little man,
not Rumpelstiltskin, at all, at all . . .
he took the fullness that love began.

Returning north, even the sky grew thin
like a high window looking nowhere.
The road was as flat as a sheet of tin.

*Somebody who should have been born*
*is gone.*

Yes, woman, such logic will lead
to loss without death.  Or say what you meant,
you coward . . . this baby that I bleed.

# WITH MERCY FOR THE GREEDY

For my friend, Ruth, who urges me to make an
appointment for the Sacrament of Confession

Concerning your letter in which you ask
me to call a priest and in which you ask
me to wear The Cross that you enclose;
your own cross,
your dog-bitten cross,
no larger than a thumb,
small and wooden, no thorns, this rose —

I pray to its shadow,
that gray place
where it lies on your letter . . . deep, deep.
I detest my sins and I try to believe
in The Cross. I touch its tender hips, its dark jawed face,
its solid neck, its brown sleep.

True. There is
a beautiful Jesus.
He is frozen to his bones like a chunk of beef.
How desperately he wanted to pull his arms in!
How desperately I touch his vertical and horizontal axes!
But I can't. Need is not quite belief.

All morning long
I have worn
your cross, hung with package string around my throat.
It tapped me lightly as a child's heart might,
tapping secondhand, softly waiting to be born.
Ruth, I cherish the letter you wrote.

My friend, my friend, I was born
doing reference work in sin, and born
confessing it.  This is what poems are:
with mercy
for the greedy,
they are the tongue's wrangle,
the world's pottage, the rat's star.

# FOR GOD WHILE SLEEPING

Sleeping in fever, I am unfit
to know just who you are:
hung up like a pig on exhibit,
the delicate wrists,
the beard drooling blood and vinegar;
hooked to your own weight,
jolting toward death under your nameplate.

Everyone in this crowd needs a bath.
I am dressed in rags.
The mother wears blue. You grind your teeth
and with each new breath
your jaws gape and your diaper sags.
I am not to blame
for all this. I do not know your name.

Skinny man, you are somebody's fault.
You ride on dark poles —
a wooden bird that a trader built
for some fool who felt
that he could make the flight. Now you roll
in your sleep, seasick
on your own breathing, poor old convict.

# IN THE DEEP MUSEUM

My God, my God, what queer corner am I in?
Didn't I die, blood running down the post,
lungs gagging for air, die there for the sin
of anyone, my sour mouth giving up the ghost?
Surely my body is done? Surely I died?
And yet, I know, I'm here. What place is this?
Cold and queer, I sting with life. I lied.
Yes, I lied. Or else in some damned cowardice
my body would not give me up. I touch
fine cloth with my hands and my cheeks are cold.
If this is hell, then hell could not be much,
neither as special nor as ugly as I was told.

What's that I hear, snuffling and pawing its way
toward me? Its tongue knocks a pebble out of place
as it slides in, a sovereign. How can I pray?
It is panting; it is an odor with a face
like the skin of a donkey. It laps my sores.
It is hurt, I think, as I touch its little head.
It bleeds. I have forgiven murderers and whores
and now I must wait like old Jonah, not dead
nor alive, stroking a clumsy animal. A rat.
His teeth test me; he waits like a good cook,
knowing his own ground. I forgive him that,
as I forgave my Judas the money he took.

Now I hold his soft red sore to my lips
as his brothers crowd in, hairy angels who take
my gift. My ankles are a flute. I lose hips
and wrists. For three days, for love's sake,

25

I bless this other death. Oh, not in air —
in dirt. Under the rotting veins of its roots,
under the markets, under the sheep bed where
the hill is food, under the slippery fruits
of the vineyard, I go. Unto the bellies and jaws
of rats I commit my prophecy and fear.
Far below The Cross, I correct its flaws.
We have kept the miracle. I will not be here.

# GHOSTS

Some ghosts are women,
neither abstract nor pale,
their breasts as limp as killed fish.
Not witches, but ghosts
who come, moving their useless arms
like forsaken servants.

Not all ghosts are women,
I have seen others;
fat, white-bellied men,
wearing their genitals like old rags.
Not devils, but ghosts.
This one thumps barefoot, lurching
above my bed.

But that isn't all.
Some ghosts are children.
Not angels, but ghosts;
curling like pink tea cups
on any pillow, or kicking,
showing their innocent bottoms, wailing
for Lucifer.

3

# THE FORTRESS

*while taking a nap with Linda*

Under the pink quilted covers
I hold the pulse that counts your blood.
I think the woods outdoors
are half asleep,
left over from summer
like a stack of books after a flood,
left over like those promises I never keep.
On the right, the scrub pine tree
waits like a fruit store
holding up bunches of tufted broccoli.

We watch the wind from our square bed.
I press down my index finger —
half in jest, half in dread —
on the brown mole
under your left eye, inherited
from my right cheek: a spot of danger
where a bewitched worm ate its way through our soul
in search of beauty. My child, since July
the leaves have been fed
secretly from a pool of beet-red dye.

And sometimes they are battle green
with trunks as wet as hunters' boots,
smacked hard by the wind, clean
as oilskins. No,
the wind's not off the ocean.

Yes, it cried in your room like a wolf
and your pony tail hurt you.  That was a long time ago.
The wind rolled the tide like a dying
woman.  She wouldn't sleep,
she rolled there all night, grunting and sighing.


Darling, life is not in my hands;
life with its terrible changes
will take you, bombs or glands,
your own child at
your breast, your own house on your own land.
Outside the bittersweet turns orange.
Before she died, my mother and I picked those fat
branches, finding orange nipples
on the gray wire strands.
We weeded the forest, curing trees like cripples.


Your feet thump-thump against my back
and you whisper to yourself.  Child,
what are you wishing?  What pact
are you making?
What mouse runs between your eyes?  What ark
can I fill for you when the world goes wild?
The woods are underwater, their weeds are shaking
in the tide; birches like zebra fish
flash by in a pack.
Child, I cannot promise that you will get your wish.


I cannot promise very much.
I give you the images I know.
Lie still with me and watch.
A pheasant moves
by like a seal, pulled through the mulch
by his thick white collar.  He's on show

like a clown.  He drags a beige feather that he removed,
one time, from an old lady's hat.
We laugh and we touch.
I promise you love.  Time will not take away that.

4

# OLD

I'm afraid of needles.
I'm tired of rubber sheets and tubes.
I'm tired of faces that I don't know
and now I think that death is starting.
Death starts like a dream,
full of objects and my sister's laughter.
We are young and we are walking
and picking wild blueberries
all the way to Damariscotta.
Oh Susan, she cried,
you've stained your new waist.
Sweet taste —
my mouth so full
and the sweet blue running out
all the way to Damariscotta.
What are you doing? Leave me alone!
Can't you see I'm dreaming?
In a dream you are never eighty.

# THE HANGMAN

Reasonable, reasonable, reasonable . . . we walked through
ten different homes, they always call them homes,
to find one ward where they like the babies who
look like you. Each time, the eyes that no one owns
watched us silently, these visitors from the street
that moves outside. They watched, but did not know
about time, there in the house where babies never grow.
My boy, though innocent and mild
your brain is obsolete.
Those six times that you almost died
the newest medicine and the family fuss
pulled you back again. Supplied
with air, against my guilty wish,
your clogged pipes cried
like Lazarus.


At first your mother said . . . why me! why me!
But she got over that. Now she enjoys
her dull daily care and her hectic bravery.
You do not love anyone. She is not growing a boy;
she is enlarging a stone to wear around her neck.
Some nights in our bed her mouth snores at me coldly
or when she turns, her kisses walking out of the sea,
I think of the bad stories,
the monster and the wreck.
I think of that Scandinavian tale
that tells of the king who killed nine

sons in turn. Slaughtered wholesale,
they had one life in common
as you have mine,
my son.

# WOMAN WITH GIRDLE

Your midriff sags toward your knees;
your breasts lie down in air,
their nipples as uninvolved
as warm starfish.
You stand in your elastic case,
still not giving up the new-born
and the old-born cycle.
Moving, you roll down the garment,
down that pink snapper and hoarder,
as your belly, soft as pudding,
slops into the empty space;
down, over the surgeon's careful mark,
down over hips, those head cushions
and mouth cushions,
slow motion like a rolling pin,
over crisp hairs, that amazing field
that hides your genuis from your patron;
over thighs, thick as young pigs,
over knees like saucers,
over calves, polished as leather,
down toward the feet.
You pause for a moment,
tying your ankles into knots.
Now you rise,
a city from the sea,
born long before Alexandria was,
straightway from God you have come
into your redeeming skin.

# THE HOUSE

In dreams
the same bad dream goes on.
Like some gigantic German toy
the house has been rebuilt
upon its kelly-green lawn.
The same dreadful set,
the same family of orange and pink faces
carved and dressed up like puppets
who wait for their jaws to open and shut.


Nineteen forty-two,
nineteen forty-three,
nineteen forty-four . . .
it's all the same. We're at war.
They've rationed the gas for all three cars.
The Lincoln Continental breathes in its stall,
a hopped up greyhound waiting to be sprung.


The Irish boy
who dated her
(lace curtain Irish, her mother said)
urges her through the lead-colored garages
to feel the patent-leather fenders
and peek at the mileage.
All that money!
and kisses too.
Kisses that stick in the mouth

like the vinegar candy she used to pull
with her buttery fingers, pull
until it was white like a dog's bone,
white, thick and impossible to chew.

Father,
an exact likeness,
his face bloated and pink
with black market scotch,
sits out his monthly bender
in his custom-made pajamas
and shouts, his tongue as quick as galloping horses,
shouts into the long distance telephone call.
His mouth is as wide as his kiss.

Mother,
with just the right gesture,
kicks her shoes off,
but is made all wrong,
impossibly frumpy as she sits there
in her alabaster dressing room
sorting her diamonds like a bank teller
to see if they add up.

The maid
as thin as a popsicle stick,
holds dinner as usual,
rubs her angry knuckles over the porcelain sink
and grumbles at the gun-shy bird dog.
She knows something is going on.
She pricks a baked potato.

The aunt,
older than all the crooked women
in *The Brothers Grimm,*
leans by a gooseneck lamp in her second floor suite,

turns up her earphone to eavesdrop
and continues to knit,
her needles working like kitchen shears
and her breasts blown out like two
pincushions.

The houseboy,
a quick-eyed Filipino,
slinks by like a Japanese spy
from French Provincial room
to French Provincial room,
emptying the ash trays and plumping up
the down upholstery.
His jacket shines, old shiny black,
a wise undertaker.

The milkman walks in his cartoon
every other day in the snoozy dawn,
rattling his bottles like a piggy bank.
And gardeners come, six at a time,
pulling petunias and hairy angel bells
up through the mulch.

This one again,
made vaguely and cruelly,
one eye green and one eye blue,
has the only major walk-on so far,
has walked from her afternoon date
past the waiting baked potatoes,
past the flashing back of the Japanese spy,
up the cotton batten stairs,
past the clicking and unclicking of the earphone,
turns here at the hall
by the diamonds that she'll never earn
and the bender that she kissed last night

among thick set stars, the floating bed
and the strange white key . . .
up like a skein of yarn,
up another flight into the penthouse,
to slam the door on all the years
she'll have to live through . . .
the sailor who she won't with,
the boys who will walk on
from Andover, Exeter and St. Marks,
the boys who will walk off with pale unlined faces,
to slam the door on all the days she'll stay the same
and never ask why and never think who to ask,
to slam the door and rip off her orange blouse.
   *Father, father, I wish I were dead.*

At thirty-five
she'll dream she's dead
or else she'll dream she's back.
All day long the house sits
larger than Russia
gleaming like a cured hide in the sun.
All day long the machine waits: rooms,
stairs, carpets, furniture, people —
those people who stand at the open windows like objects
waiting to topple.

# WATER

We are fisherman in a flat scene.
All day long we are in love with water.
The fish are naked.
The fish are always awake.
They are the color of old spoons
and caramels.
The sun reaches down
but the floor is not in sight.
Only the rocks are white and green.
Who knows what goes on in the halls below?

It's queer to meet the loon falling in
across the top of the yellow lake
like a checkered hunchback
dragging his big feet.
Only his head and neck can breathe.
He yodels.
He goes under yodeling
like the first mate
who sways all night in his hammock, calling
        I have seen, I have seen.

    Water is worse than woman.
    It calls to a man to empty him.
    Under us
    twelve princesses dance all night,
    exhausting their lovers, then giving them up.
    I have known water.
    I have sung all night

for the last cargo of boys.
I have sung all night
for the mouths that float back later,
one by one,
holding a lady's wornout shoe.

# WALLFLOWER

Come friend,
I have an old story to tell you —

Listen.
Sit down beside me and listen.
My face is red with sorrow
and my breasts are made of straw.
I sit in the ladder-back chair
in a corner of the polished stage.
I have forgiven all the old actors for dying.
A new one comes on with the same lines,
like large white growths, in his mouth.
The dancers come on from the wings,
perfectly mated.

I look up. The ceiling is pearly.
My thighs press, knotting in their treasure.
Upstage the bride falls in satin to the floor.
Beside her the tall hero in a red wool robe
stirs the fire with his ivory cane.
The string quartet plays for itself,
gently, gently, sleeves and waxy bows.
The legs of the dancers leap and catch.
I myself have little stiff legs,
my back is as straight as a book
and how I came to this place —
the little feverish roses,
the islands of olives and radishes,
the blissful pastimes of the parlor —
I'll never know.

# HOUSEWIFE

Some women marry houses.
It's another kind of skin; it has a heart,
a mouth, a liver and bowel movements.
The walls are permanent and pink.
See how she sits on her knees all day,
faithfully washing herself down.
Men enter by force, drawn back like Jonah
into their fleshy mothers.
A woman *is* her mother.
That's the main thing.

# DOORS, DOORS, DOORS

## 1. *Old Man*

Old man, it's four flights up and for what?
Your room is hardly any bigger than your bed.
Puffing as you climb, you are a brown woodcut
stooped over the thin rail and the wornout tread.

The room will do.  All that's left of the old life
is jampacked on shelves from floor to ceiling
like a supermarket: your books, your dead wife
generously fat in her polished frame, the congealing

bowl of cornflakes sagging in their instant milk,
your hot plate and your one luxury, a telephone.
You leave your door open, lounging in maroon silk
and smiling at the other roomers who live alone.
Well, almost alone.  Through the old-fashioned wall
the fellow next door has a girl who comes to call.

Twice a week at noon during their lunch hour
they pause by your door to peer into your world.
They speak sadly as if the wine they carry would sour
or as if the mattress would not keep them curled

together, extravagantly young in their tight lock.
Old man, you are their father holding court
in the dingy hall until their alarm clock
rings and unwinds them.  You unstopper the quart

of brandy you've saved, examining the small print
in the telephone book. The phone in your lap is all
that's left of your family name. Like a Romanoff prince
you stay the same in your small alcove off the hall.
Castaway, your time is a flat sea that doesn't stop,
with no new land to make for and no new stories to swap.


## 2. *Seamstress*

I'm at pains to know what else I could have done
but move out of his parish, him being my son;

him being the only one at home since his Pa
left us to beat the Japs at Okinawa.

I put the gold star up in the front window
beside the flag. Alterations is what I know

and what I did: hems, gussets and seams.
When my boy had the fever and the bad dreams

I paid for the clinic exam and a pack of lies.
As a youngster his private parts were undersize.

I thought of his Pa, that muscly old laugh he had
and the boy was thin as a moth, but never once bad,

as smart as a rooster! To hear some neighbors tell,
Your kid! He'll go far. He'll marry well.

So when he talked of taking the cloth, I thought
I'd talk him out of it. You're all I got,

I told him. For six years he studied up. I prayed
against God Himself for my boy. But he stayed.

Christ was a hornet inside his head. I guess
I'd better stitch the zipper in this dress.

I guess I'll get along. I always did.
Across the hall from me's an old invalid,

aside of him, a young one — he carries on
with a girl who pretends she comes to use the john.

The old one with bad breath and his bed all mussed,
he smiles and talks to them. He's got some crust.

Sure as hell, what else could I have done
but pack up and move in here, him being my son?


3. *Young Girl*

Dear love, as simple as some distant evil
we walk a little drunk up these three flights
where you tacked a Dufy print above your army cot.

The thin apartment doors on the way up will
not tell on us. We are saying, we have *our* rights
and let them see the sandwiches and wine we bought

for we do not explain my husband's insane abuse
and we do not say why your wild-haired wife has fled
or that my father opened like a walnut and then was dead.
Your palms fold over me like knees. Love is the only use.

51

Both a little drunk in the middle afternoon
with the forgotten smart of August on our skin
we hold hands as if we still were children who trudge

up the wooden tower, on up past that close platoon
of doors, past the dear old man who always asks us in
and the one who sews like a wasp and will not budge.

Climbing the dark halls, I ignore their papers and pails,
the twelve coats of rubbish of someone else's dim life.
Tell them need is an excuse for love. Tell them need prevails.
Tell them I remake and smooth your bed and am your wife.

5

For Comfort
who was actually my grandfather

# LETTER WRITTEN ON A FERRY WHILE
# CROSSING LONG ISLAND SOUND

I am surprised to see
that the ocean is still going on.
Now I am going back
and I have ripped my hand
from your hand as I said I would
and I have made it this far
as I said I would
and I am on the top deck now
holding my wallet, my cigarettes
and my car keys
at 2 o'clock on a Tuesday
in August of 1960.

Dearest,
although everything has happened,
nothing has happened.
The sea is very old.
The sea is the face of Mary,
without miracles or rage
or unusual hope,
grown rough and wrinkled
with incurable age.

Still,
I have eyes.
These are my eyes:
the orange letters that spell

ORIENT on the life preserver
that hangs by my knees;
the cement lifeboat that wears
its dirty canvas coat;
the faded sign that sits on its shelf
saying KEEP OFF.
Oh, all right, I say,
I'll save myself.


Over my right shoulder
I see four nuns
who sit like a bridge club,
their faces poked out
from under their habits,
as good as good babies who
have sunk into their carriages.
Without discrimination
the wind pulls the skirts
of their arms.
Almost undressed,
I see what remains:
that holy wrist,
that ankle,
that chain.


Oh God,
although I am very sad,
could you please
let these four nuns
loosen from their leather boots
and their wooden chairs
to rise out
over this greasy deck,

56

out over this iron rail,
nodding their pink heads to one side,
flying four abreast
in the old-fashioned side stroke;
each mouth open and round,
breathing together
as fish do,
singing without sound.


Dearest,
see how my dark girls sally forth,
over the passing lighthouse of Plum Gut,
its shell as rusty
as a camp dish,
as fragile as a pagoda
on a stone;
out over the little lighthouse
that warns me of drowning winds
that rub over its blind bottom
and its blue cover;
winds that will take the toes
and the ears of the rider
or the lover.


There go my dark girls,
their dresses puff
in the leeward air.
Oh, they are lighter than flying dogs
or the breath of dolphins;
each mouth opens gratefully,
wider than a milk cup.
My dark girls sing for this.
They are going up.

57

See them rise
on black wings, drinking
the sky, without smiles
or hands
or shoes.
They call back to us
from the gauzy edge of paradise,
*good news, good news.*

# FROM THE GARDEN

Come, my beloved,
consider the lilies.
We are of little faith.
We talk too much.
Put your mouthful of words away
and come with me to watch
the lilies open in such a field,
growing there like yachts,
slowly steering their petals
without nurses or clocks.
Let us consider the view:
a house where white clouds
decorate the muddy halls.
Oh, put away your good words
and your bad words. Spit out
your words like stones!
Come here! Come here!
Come eat my pleasant fruits.

# LOVE SONG FOR K. OWYNE

*When I lay down for death*
*my love came down to Craigy's Sea*
*and fished me from the snakes.*
*He let me use his breath.*
*He pushed away the mud and lay with me.*
*And lay with me in sin.*


I washed lobster and stale gin
off your shirt. We lived in sin
in too many rooms. Now you live in Ohio
among the hard fields of potatoes,
the gray sticks and the bad breath
of the coal mines. Oh Love, you know
how the waves came running up the stairs
for me, just as the nervous trees
in Birnam wood crept up upon Macbeth
to catch his charmed head turning and well aware.
I was not safe. I heard the army in the sea
move in, again and again, against me.


Shuffled between caring and disgrace
I took up all our closet space.
What luxury we first checked into,
to growl like lawyers until I threw
my diamonds and cash upon the floor.
You'd come for death. I couldn't suit you
until the sun came up as mild as a pear

and the room, having hurt us, was ours.
You sang me a song about bones, dinosaur
bones.  Though I was bony you found me fair.
In the bay, the imported swans drank for hours
like pale acrobats or gently drunken flowers.

# FLIGHT

Thinking that I would find you,
thinking I would make the plane
that goes hourly out of Boston
I drove into the city.
Thinking that on such a night
every thirsty man would have his jug
and that the Negro women would lie down
on pale sheets and even the river into town
would stretch out naturally on its couch,
I drove into the city.
On such a night, at the end of the river,
the airport would sputter with planes
like ticker-tape.

Foot on the gas
I sang aloud to the front seat,
to the clumps of women in cotton dresses,
to the patches of fog crusting the banks,
and to the sailboats swinging on their expensive hooks.
There was rose and violet on the river
as I drove through the mist into the city.
I was full of letters I hadn't sent you,
a red coat over my shoulders
and new white gloves in my lap.

I dropped through the city
as the river does,
rumbling over and under, as indicated,
past the miles of spotted windows

minding their own business,
through the Sumner Tunnel,
trunk by trunk through its sulphurous walls,
tile by tile like a men's urinal,
slipping through
like somebody else's package.

Parked, at last,
on a dime that would never last,
I ran through the airport.
Wild for love, I ran through the airport,
stockings and skirts and dollars.
The night clerk yawned all night at the public,
his mind on tomorrow's wages.
All flights were grounded.
The planes sat and the gulls sat,
heavy and rigid in a pool of glue.

Knowing I would never find you
I drove out of the city.
At the airport one thousand cripples
sat nursing a sore foot.
There was more fog
and the rain came down when it thought of it.
I drove past the eye and ear infirmaries,
past the office buildings lined up like dentures,
and along Storrow Drive the streetlights
sucked in all the insects who
had nowhere else to go.

# FOR ELEANOR BOYLAN TALKING WITH GOD

God has a brown voice,
as soft and full as beer.
Eleanor, who is more beautiful than my mother,
is standing in her kitchen talking
and I am breathing in my cigarettes like poison.
She stands in her lemon-colored sun dress
motioning to God with her wet hands
glossy from the washing of egg plates.
She tells him! She tells him like a drunk
who doesn't need to see to talk.
It's casual but friendly.
God is as close as the ceiling.

Though no one can ever know,
I don't think he has a face.
He had a face when I was six and a half.
Now he is large, covering up the sky
like a great resting jellyfish.
When I was eight I thought the dead people
stayed up there like blimps.
Now my chair is as hard as a scarecrow
and outside the summer flies sing like a choir.
Eleanor, before he leaves tell him . . .
Oh Eleanor, Eleanor,
tell him before death uses you up.

# THE BLACK ART

A woman who writes feels too much,
those trances and portents!
As if cycles and children and islands
weren't enough; as if mourners and gossips
and vegetables were never enough.
She thinks she can warn the stars.
A writer is essentially a spy.
Dear love, I am that girl.

A man who writes knows too much,
such spells and fetiches!
As if erections and congresses and products
weren't enough; as if machines and galleons
and wars were never enough.
With used furniture he makes a tree.
A writer is essentially a crook.
Dear love, you are that man.

Never loving ourselves,
hating even our shoes and our hats,
we love each other, *precious, precious.*
Our hands are light blue and gentle.
Our eyes are full of terrible confessions.
But when we marry,
the children leave in disgust.
There is too much food and no one left over
to eat up all the weird abundance.

# LETTER WRITTEN DURING A JANUARY NORTHEASTER

## Monday

Dearest,
It is snowing, grotesquely snowing,
upon the small faces of the dead.
Those dear loudmouths, gone for over a year,
buried side by side
like little wrens.
But why should I complain?
The dead turn over casually,
thinking ...
        Good! No visitors today.
My window, which is not a grave,
is dark with my fierce concentration
and too much snowing
and too much silence.
The snow has quietness in it; no songs,
no smells, no shouts or traffic.
When I speak
my own voice shocks me.

## Tuesday

I have invented a lie.
There is no other day but Monday.
It seemed reasonable to pretend
that I could change the day
like a pair of socks.
To tell the truth
days are all the same size
and words aren't much company.

If I were sick, I'd be a child,
tucked in under the woolens, sipping my broth.
As it is,
the days are not worth grabbing or lying about.
Nevertheless, you are the only one
that I can bother with this matter.


### Monday

It would be pleasant to be drunk:
faithless to my tongue and hands,
giving up the boundaries
for the heroic gin.
Dead drunk
is the term I think of,
insensible,
neither cool nor warm,
without a head or a foot.
To be drunk is to be intimate with a fool.
I will try it shortly.


### Monday

Just yesterday,
twenty-eight men aboard a damaged radar tower
foundered down seventy miles off the coast.
Immediately their hearts slammed shut.
The storm would not cough them up.
Today they are whispering over Sonar.
Small voice,
what do you say?
Aside from the going down, the awful wrench,
the pulleys and hooks and the black tongue . . .
What are your headquarters?
Are they kind?

## Monday

It must be Friday by now.
I admit I have been lying.
Days don't freeze
and to say that the snow has quietness in it
is to ignore the possibilities of the word.
Only the tree has quietness in it;
quiet as the crucifix,
pounded out years ago
like a handmade shoe.
Someone once
told an elephant to stand still.
That's why trees remain quiet all winter.
They're not going anywhere.

## Monday

Dearest,
where are your letters?
The mailman is an impostor.
He is actually my grandfather.
He floats far off in the storm
with his nicotine mustache and a bagful of nickels.
His legs stumble through
baskets of eyelashes.
Like all the dead
he picks up his disguise,
shakes it off and slowly pulls down the shade,
fading out like an old movie.
Now he is gone
as you are gone.
But he belongs to me like lost baggage.